MW00887671

Poems of Inspiration!
From Genesis To Revelation

Reginald Love

authorHOUSE®

AuthorHouse™
1663 Liberty Drive
Bloomington, IN 47403
www.authorhouse.com
Phone: 1-800-839-8640

© *2009 Reginald Love. All rights reserved.*

No part of this book may be reproduced, stored in a retrieval system, or transmitted by any means without the written permission of the author.

First published by AuthorHouse 12/30/2009

ISBN: 978-1-4490-5575-2 (e)
ISBN: 978-1-4490-5573-8 (sc)

Library of Congress Control Number: 2009913063

Printed in the United States of America
Bloomington, Indiana

This book is printed on acid-free paper.

Dedication

This book is dedicated to God, the creator and maker of all things. It is also dedicated to my mother, Gloria Love, my father, Claud Love and my grandmother, Vinie Johnson, who we all called Big Mama. These three people taught me about God from the time that I was a little boy, until I graduated from high school. I disregarded their teachings after graduating from high school and lived a wild life. But, there were two things they taught me, that always stayed in the back of my mind, "God parted the Red Sea and raised Jesus from the dead". So when I thought I was about to die one day, I did not call 911 or friends, but called on that God. Many other people were an inspiration to me, relatives, teachers, coaches and members of the church, but I truly believe that had it not been for the teachings of my Mother, Father and Big Mama, that I would be dead and sleeping in my grave. My Mother was an Usher, who emphasized education, while my Father was a Deacon, that stressed hard work, and Big Mama quoted scriptures every day. I didn't appreciate it when I was young, but looking back now, this was quite a combination! Reginald Love :)

Table of Contents

The Church And Me

People search the world over, for mountain peaks that crest the sky,
But upon leaving, their souls , it did not satisfy.
Many spend a lifetime, seeking riches, fortune and fame,
Forsaking friends, family and loved ones, what a shame!
Families shouldn't turn a deaf ear, to a family member's plea
Remember Paul says its our duty, The Church and Me.
When a friend is down and their way they can not see,
Who'll be there to help them if not the Church and me?
No matter should I travel as far as the eyes can see,
May I never forget, The Church is in me!
Because for some, the church doors, they have yet to cross,
If they can't see the church in me, I'm guilty of their loss!
Christians shouldn't just leave their Bibles on the shelf,
But read what it says, "Love your neighbor as yourself."
While waiting in line, be kind, patient, and cool,
These are things you should have learned in Sunday School☺
So before we blame the economy, newspapers, and TV,
Take time to remember, "The Church is in me."
When you see someone down, don't just point to Calvary,
Lend them a hand and remember , the Church is in me.
When I grow old, steps have slowed , and all my hair is gray,
Hope some young person with a smile, will brighten my day.
And remind me, I didn't forget your poem , you see,
I shall never forget, I remember " The Church is in Me."

By Reginald Love
October 2005

1

The Creation

There was nothing to watch, and nothing to see,
God merely spoke, and the world came to be!
God said, "Let there be light," because he could,
Then the almighty saw that it was good.
Then God separated light from dark,
For the first day, not a bad start!
Then God separated waters above from waters below,
This must have been quite a show!
Then God called the space, sky I say,
This happened on the second day.
Then God without even waving his hand,
Created the oceans and dry land!
God said, "let the land burst forth with grass, plants and trees,
With each one producing like bearing seeds."
Not a fairy tale, it happened just this way,
And this was just the third day.
On the fourth day God showed his might,
Created the sun for day and the moon for night!
The fifth day proves the big bang theory a lie,
God created the fish in the sea, and the birds in the sky!
Then God created wildlife, any animal you can find,
With each being able to reproduce its own kind.
On the sixth day, came a very big plan,
God said, "Let us make man."
As humble as it might sound,
Man was formed from the dust of the ground.
God breathed into his nostrils, I'm told,
And man became a living soul!

9-19-09

2

Adam And Eve

When the making of all the animals was done,
God brought them to Adam to name each one.
Animals are creatures not to abandon,
But Adam himself, needed a companion.
God caused Adam to fall into a deep sleep,
Then made from his rib, a companion to keep.
Adam awoke and was pleased with God's plan,
Adam said, "She's part of me and called her wo' man.
From the tree of knowledge, Adam and Eve were not to eat,
But the serpent was shrewd, and full of deceit.
The serpent then called God a lie,
Told Eve, "You shall not surely die."
The serpent said, "God knows it will open your eyes,
And you will be like God, all knowing and wise."
So the woman went ahead and did eat some,
Then Adam ate, after she gave him one.
Their eyes opened, they knew nakedness and shame,
Since then, things have never been the same. ☺
Adam blamed the woman, she blamed the snake,
Their wrongdoing seriously affected mankind's fate.
God told the serpent, "Since you caused this strife,
You will crawl on your belly the rest of your life."
Then God told the woman, simple and plain,
"You will bear children and suffer in pain."
God told Adam, "You listened to her over me, this I can't allow
From now on you will live from the sweat of your brow."
This was a hard lesson to have to learn,
God said, "From dust you came and dust you shall return."

9-21-09

Noah

Mankind had become such a disgrace,
God decided to destroy the human race.
Morality, people would totally disregard,
But Noah found favor with the Lord.
It had never rained on the earth before,
But now God was going to make it pour!
God said, "Build an ark from gopher wood,"
So Noah did the best he could.
God said, "Make it four hundred and fifty feet long,
Seventy five feet wide, forty five feet high and strong."
Then God told Noah what more to do,
"Bring in each kind of animal, two by two."
Noah had one week to get everyone on board,
He managed it, because his family was on one accord.
Water burst from the earth and fell from the sky,
Now all would know that Noah did not lie.
Can you imagine on earth, all the fright?
It rained for forty days and forty nights!
Because the people didn't follow God's ways,
Water covered the earth for one hundred and fifty days!
Noah sent a raven and a dove to fly around,
To see if the waters had gone down.
The third time the dove did not come back,
Then Noah knew the water was down in fact.
God said, "When you see the rainbow that I send,
It's a sign, I will not destroy by water again."

9-21-09

4

Abraham

While no one could open the book but the Lamb,
Christians everywhere owe a lot to Father Abraham!
The lord told Abram to pick up his things and go,
Where he was going , he did not know.
This set the stage, since his father was not alive,
And Abram himself was now seventy five!
Because of his Faith, he didn't even ask why?
God said, " Your descendents will out number the stars in the sky."
Abram told lot, "we're relatives, we shouldn't fight."
Choose the land you want, to the left or to the right.
Lot chose the land between Sodom and Gomorrah,
A place full of evil, greed, and horror.
God was ready to destroy the city,
Abram asked, if he found fifty, to show pity.
But in Sodom and Gomorrah, there was so much sin,
Abram couldn't find ten good men!
As the city burned, God said, " Don't look back."
But Lots wife, for some reason, didn't heed that.
She looked back, it was no one else's fault,
Lot's wife turned into a pillar of salt!
Abram was willing to sacrifice his only son,
God knew then, he'd chosen the right one!
Abraham always kept God, within his reach,
God said, "Your descendents will outnumber sands on the beach."
If you believe in the God of Abraham,
You are one of his descendents, just as I am!

8-11-09

6

Isaac

Abraham was one hundred, plain as can be,
Going to have a son? God your kidding me!
Sarah was ninety, barren, with no son,
God said, "Now I'm going to give you one!"
Sarah laughed ☺ because of her age,
But God said , " Your son will be all the rage!"
Then after awhile, in fact sometime after,
Isaac was born, his name meaning laughter☺
Isaac thought they were going to sacrifice a ram,
He said, "I see the fire and wood, where's the lamb?"
Isaac didn't resist being tied down as a sacrifice,
Then watched , as his father drew his knife.
The death of Isaac would have been sad,
An angel appeared and said, " Don't hurt the lad."
Abraham was not one to question, rush or push,
Looked, and behold! There was a ram in the bush!
Isaac listened and led an obedient life,
Even allowed Rebecca to be his chosen wife.
Isaac for some reason, was God's chosen one,
But he and Rebecca would have two sons.
One of the sons would dream about a ladder,
The CHOSEN one would be called Jacob the Grabber.

8-12-09
Reginald Love

Jacob

Rebecca was barren, nothing had come from her womb,
But Isaac pleaded with God and she conceived soon.
Rebecca felt inside her there was a struggle,
So she asked God, "What was the trouble?"
God said , "There are two nations inside you, no wonder."
They will separate, but the older will serve the younger.
Esau came in from the field, hungry as he could be,
He said to Jacob, "Feed me some pottage, I pray thee."
Jacob could see he was very hungry alright,
So he told Esau, "Sell me your birthright."
Esau was about to die, starving more or less,
Said, "What good is a birthright? If I starve to death.
So Esau sold his birthright for a mess of pottage,
And became like a circuit, that's lost its wattage.
Rebecca sent Jacob to his uncle Labon to stay,
Leah had pretty eyes, but Rachel pretty, shapely in every way!
Jacob was excited to be starting a new life,
He said , "I'll work seven years for Rachel to be my wife."
But according to the custom, as was back then,
When time was up, Leah not Rachel was brought in!
Jacob was disappointed, probably almost in tears,
Said, "For Rachel, I'll work another seven years."
Jacob was prosperous, busy and had twelve sons ☺
Joseph, the one by Rachel would be the CHOSEN one.
Jacob wrestled the angel, all night we know,
Then told the angel, "Bless me before you go."
The angel said, "What is thy name? do tell,
It is Jacob no more, but now, Israel!

8-13-09

8

Joseph

Joseph had a dream, that put brothers' love to the test,
His Sheave stood taller than all the rest.
In another dream that was no less dim,
The sun, moon and eleven stars bowed before him.
They were going to kill Joseph, instead, put him in a cave,
Then for twenty pieces of silver, he was sold as a slave.
The master's wife pursued Joseph, day after day,
But God fearing Joseph would give her no play.
One day she grabbed his coat, but he did escape,
Not to be outdone, she then cried rape!
Thrown in prison, things looked very dark,
But God was with him, and knew his heart.
The butler had a dream, he did not understand,
He didn't know he was in prison with God's man.
In prison Joseph continued God's ways,
He told the butler, "you will be restored in three days."
The butler was happy that he was going to be free,
Joseph told him, " don't forget about me."
Seven fat cows, seven skinny cows in Pharaoh's dream,
No one could understand, what did it mean?
Like many who forget where they have been,
The butler told the king, "I remember my sin."
Joseph said, "there's going to be a famine in the land,
For seven years, store up all you can."
Pharaoh said, "because your interpretation is true,
In Egypt, I alone shall out rank you."
Joseph then forgave his brothers,
And told them to go back and get the others.
To Egypt, Jacob did not want to go,
But years later, Moses would say, "let my people go!"

8-18-09

Moses

Moses was tending sheep, and did not know what loomed,
When he saw a bush burning, that was not consumed.
Moses saw no one, but heard a voice sound,
God said, "Take off your shoes, you're on holy ground."
God said, "I've heard the wails of the people and lo,"
Go tell Pharaoh to let my people go.
Moses gave Pharaoh signs from God and clues,
As for letting the people go, he refused.
Moses said, "In Egypt, even where everyone lies,
Will be covered with swarms of flies."
Pharaoh said, "Ok, go worship your God, I don't care,"
Just get all of these flies out of the air!
Then God sent plagues of a different kind,
Time after time, Pharaoh would change his mind.
Then God in heaven, who sits high and looks low,
Said, "When I kill the firstborn, he'll let you go."
When on their door, God saw the blood,
They were spared, like Noah during the flood.
The miracles were like thunder or a lightening rod,
So generation to generation, will know who is God.
At the Red Sea, there was much grumbling and discord,
Moses said, "Stand back and watch the salvation of the Lord!"
The people watched as Moses held out his rod,
Then the Red Sea parted, and they praised God!
Moses did his best to carry out God's plan,
Allowed to see, but not enter the promised land.
Only Joshua and Caleb brought back a good report,
The others didn't believe and were out of sort.
After all the doubt, blood, sweat, and tears,
They were forced to wander for forty years.

8-19-09

10

Balaam

The children of Israel were now many,
As they approached, the Moabites were scared plenty!
They thought things were about to get worse,
So on Israel, they asked Balaam to curse.
When Balaam told God about the whole mess,
God said, "you can't curse them, they're blessed."☺
When Balaam told them what God had said,
They sent others to talk to him instead.
Balaam said, "even if you give me a house of silver and gold."
I must obey God, and do what I'm told.
The next day, as Balaam rode, looking at the land,
His donkey saw an angel, sword drawn in hand.
The death angel, Balaam did not see,
His concern now, was making more money.
The donkey stopped, but Balaam didn't laugh,
As he smote the Ass with his staff.
Balaam tried to move too fast,
Then God opened the mouth of the Ass!
The Ass said, " What have I done to thee?
That with thy staff, thou would smite me."
Then God opened Balaam's eyes,
He saw the death angel, to his surprise.
Don't get caught up in the world's ways,
Remember Balaam and do what God says! ☺

8-20-09

Joshua

If God is with you, you got it made in the shade!
God told Joshua, "Don't you be afraid."
Joshua was faithful from the start,
And like the Red Sea, the Jordan would now part!
The Children of Israel crossed over a dry span,
It was time to take the promised land.
To battle against God is not sensible,
The city of Jericho was considered invincible.
But on the seventh day at the trumpets sound,
The people shouted and the walls came down!
Allowing some fighting to come to a cease,
With Gibeon, Joshua did make peace.
But five nations rose against, like drones,
And God killed them with hailstones!
As many Amorites tried to get away,
Joshua prayed to the Lord that day.
The sun and the moon, almost a day, stood still!
Because of Joshua's prayer and God's will.
If someone killed a person by accident,
To a city of refuge, they were sent.
Joshua's words were straight, not a curve,
He said,"Choose you this day, who you will serve."
Joshua's family was on one accord,
He said, "As for me and my house, we will serve the Lord."

8-21-09

Rahab

Rahab was a lady of the evening, you see,
But she heard about the parting of the Red Sea.
The two spies lodged at the harlot's place,
The enemy would not get to see their face.
Despite her previous life's affairs,
Her faith told her to hide them upstairs.
Rahab said , "We heard how you conquered the other land."
There's no courage left here in any man!
Rahab said, "This one thing I know,
Your God is God in heaven and below."
Rahab said, "Since I'm saving your life this time,
When you take the city, it's only fair you spare mine."
The spies said, "Ok, just don't tell what we're doing,"
For they knew the enemy would be pursuing.
"Hang this scarlet rope, they told her to do,
We will remember our promise to you."
God spared Rahab's family and forgave her sins,
But that's not where the story ends.
Because of her faith, she was able to save others,
And she became King David's great, great, grandmother!

8-22-09

Gideon

Gideon was thrashing wheat, he was not a loafer,
When an angel appeared by the oak in Oprah.
The angel called him a mighty man of valour,
But Gideon thought he was the least and a bit shallow.
Gideon passed his first test,
By laying Baal's alter to rest!
Gideon said, "Make the fleece wet, ground dry, so I can see,
Then I will know that God is with me.
Gideon said, "Don't be angry for now, what I ask of you,
Let the fleece be dry and the ground have dew."
Gideon's men numbered 32,000, a plenty,
But God said , "That's way too many!"
To prove that he was not wrong,
God said, "Tell the scared ones to go home."
Twenty two thousand, went home that day, ☺
They were afraid, didn't want to fight anyway.
God said, "Bring them down to the river bend,
The ones that lap like a dog, will be your men."
This left only three hundred, to do the job,
But no problem for the true and living God.
Gideon now wasn't sure what to do,
God said, "Go to their camp, see what they say about you."
A man told about a dream of a big loaf of barley bread,
Crushing the Midianites, killing them dead.
Hearing this, Gideon then rushed back,
Gathered his men for a night attack.
Confused when they heard the trumpet bellows,
The Midianites started killing their own fellows!
Let this be a lesson to all who read,
You don't need many, if you let God lead.

8-23-09

15

Samson

The Philistines held Israel like ransom,
Until God decided to send Samson.
Manoah was indeed barren alright,
The angel told her she would bear a Nazirite.
No strong drink or unclean food, she was to be fed,
And no razor was to come upon his head.
Samson's riddle, "Out of the eater came meat and sweets,
Solve it and I will give you thirty garments or sheets.
The men threatened Samson's wife,
Said they would take her fathers life.
She enticed Samson and kept leaning,
He gave in and told her the meaning.
Samson returned with garments, he promised to rend,
But they had given his wife to his friend.
To show how disappointment feels,
He tied foxes together and burned their fields.
The Israelites bound him , to turn him over,
But the spirit was on him and the ropes broke like clover.
And before this day would pass,
Samson killed one thousand with the jawbone of an ass!
Samson and Deliah were having an affair,
She found out the secret was in his hair.
With his hair cut off, his strength was gone,
They put out his eyes and made him push the grindstone.
At a Philistine party for Dagon, their god of sort,
They said, "Bring out Samson, so we can make sport."
Samson was placed between two pillar towers,
He then asked God to show his power.
Samson didn't ask for a lot of times,
"Just this once, let me die with the Philistines."
For his two eyes, he wanted to even the score,
So in his death, he killed more than ever before!

8-24-09

16

Ruth

Naomi's husband and two sons died,
Her and her two daughter in laws cried.
Naomi urged Ruth to go back to her homeland,
But Ruth said, "No with you, I will make my stand."
Even though Naomi continued to prod,
Ruth said, "Your people, my people, your God, my God."
Ruth declared with all her breath,
Nothing will separate us but death!
Ruth asked to work in the fields, no fun ☹
But Boaz saw her and said, "I've heard what you've done."
"You left your people to help Naomi," Boaz stressed,
From the God of Israel, you shall be blessed!
Naomi had sold her piece of land in fact,
Boaz saw his chance to buy it back.
And to avoid any trouble or scandal,
In front of witnesses, Boaz took off his sandal.
This transaction was nothing but the truth,
It was also the redeeming of Ruth!
Ruth and Boaz were blessed as the elders had said,
They gave birth to a son, named Obed.
Because of what she had done for another,
Ruth became king David's Great Grandmother!

8-30-09

Samuel

God spoke to Samuel from heaven above,
Awakened from his sleep, he didn't know who it was.
God said, "Tell Eli I know what's been done,
I'm going to punish him and his sons."
The Philistines captured the Ark as part of the spoils,
But the God of Israel, made them break out with boils!
Their Elder said, "make five gold tumors and five gold rats,
Hitch two cows never yoked and send the Ark back.
With the Ark, the Philistines had become annoyed,
With its return to Israel, the people were overjoyed!
"If you are serious about turning back to God, without fail,
Get rid of your idol gods, including Baal."
Samuel's praying for Israel, did not cease,
Till God heard his cry and gave Israel peace.
Samuel grew old and appointed his sons,
But unlike him, they were evil ones.
The people became upset and wanted a king,
Samuel warned them about what that would mean.
"You'll be taxed, young men as soldiers, will have to be brave,
He'll take a tenth of your flocks and make you slaves."
But the people wouldn't listen, it would seem,
They said, "Even so, we still want a king."

9-1-09

Hannah

Because no children Hannah had yet to bare,
Each year Peninnah would make fun and stare.
The tauting went on for many years,
Till Hannah wouldn't eat and shed many tears.
Hannah and her husband were not on one accord,
But Hannah took her petition to the Lord!
She cried, "Look down on my sorrow: this I promise to do,
Give me a son and I will give him back to you!"
Yours for a lifetime, he will strut,
Dedicated to God, his hair will never be cut."
The priest saw her lips moving, but heard no sound,
Eli thought she was drunk and hell bound.
"Oh no sir! I was praying to God, doing my best,"
Eli said, "In that case, may God grant your request."
Oh thank you sir! And she became glad,☺
Went back and began to eat, no longer sad.
The Lord did not forget what Hannah had done,
And in due time, gave her a son.
Hannah kept her promise and avoided debackle,
When Samuel was weaned, took him to the tabernackle.
Because of her faith and what she had done,
The Lord gave Hannah two daughters and three sons!

9-1-09

Eli

The priest's life was becoming like an evil song,
His two sons were continually doing wrong.
They were causing Eli much strife,
As they would even steal a sacrifice.
Eli's sons went so far as to even seduce,
Young women at the tabernacle for God's use.
Eli warned, "For sins against others I can plead,
But for sins against God? Who can intercede?
God said, "Because you let your sons act like beast,
Your family can no longer serve as my priest."
"To prove it is true what I say,
I will cause both sons to die on the same day!"
Eli heard his sons were killed, ark captured, Israel in a wreck,
He then fell backwards and broke his neck.
Eli was ninety eight, his sons had caused him many tears,
He had led Israel for forty years.

9-1-09

Saul

One day Kish's donkeys strayed away,
So he sent his son, Saul to save the day.
Where the donkeys were, was not clear,
So Saul went to talk to God's seer.
Samuel said, "Don't worry, the donkeys are found,
But on your head , there shall be a crown."
Saul said, "I'm from the smallest tribe, I'm not able,"
But Samuel placed him at the head of the table!
Finding a king was not easy, some feared,
Saul was chosen, but he had disappeared.
They asked God, because situation looked rough,
God said, "He's hiding among the stuff."
So they brought him out, so he could be seen,
Then Saul, officially became Israel's king.
Saul's impatience caused him much strife,
He failed to wait for Samuel to sacrifice.
Saul kept the spoils, as Israel fought for its life,
But Samuel said, "Obedience is better than sacrifice."
If Saul was tormented by God, during the day,
He asked David to play his harp, and it went away.
Saul prayed, no answer, God cut him no slack,
So he resorted to witchcraft and brought Samuel back.
Samuel said, "Why you bring me back? Nothing I can do,
God in heaven has turned against you."
What's more, tomorrow this shall come to be,
You and your sons will be here with me.
Fighting a losing battle, forsaken by the Lord,
Saul took his own life, by falling on his sword.

9-2-09

David

God told Samuel, "Stop morning for what Saul had done,
Fill your horn with oil, and go anoint Jesse's son."
Samuel looked, but it was not for him to decide,
God said, "You look outward, but I look inside."
None of the seven did God seek,
Jesse said, "I have one more, tending sheep."
Samuel poured oil on David's head,
Then the Spirit with him tread.
For forty days, Goliath mocked the Israelites,
Challenging anyone of them to a fight.
They all thought David was too young, not aware,
That David had killed a lion and a bear!
No armor, with only five stones, David went out afresh,
Told Goliath, "I'll cut off your head, the birds will eat your flesh."
With a single stone and sling, he did what he said,
David killed Goliath, and then cut off his head!
David's fame throughout the land, grew and grew,
Saul became so jealous, he didn't know what to do!
Saul's death had been long for seen,
David then became Israel's king.
But David did arouse God's wrath,
He awoke and saw Bathsheba taking a bath.
Who was she? David did infer,
Had her brought to him, and slept with her.
She became pregnant, lust had run amuck,
Then David began to plot a coverup.
But Uriah stood firm and would not rattle,
So David had him killed in battle.
In a parable, Nathan told David, shame on you!
This evil, you did not have to do.
God said, "This behavior, I despise,
Now in public, others will sleep with your wives."

Within his own family, adultery , murder and rape,
From this punishment, David could not escape.
David was forgiven however,
And God's covenant with him, lasts forever.
Samuel had said it from the start
David was a man after God's own heart.

9-3-09

DAVID SLAYING GOLIATH.

Soloman

After Soloman was named king,
God appeared to him in a dream!
God said, "Ask for whatever you might,
And it shall be granted tonight!
Soloman had no desire for riches or evil,
But he did ask for wisdom to lead the people.
"You didn't ask for death to enemies or long life for you,
God said, "Because of that, I shall give it all to you."
Soloman had to show wisdom, in a very short while,
As two prostitutes argued over a child.
Soloman said, "Lets cut the baby in two,"
But the real mother said, "That won't do!"
Throughout all the nations, Soloman's wisdom was heard,
He wrote one thousand songs and three thousand proverbs!
The Queen of Sheba came to test Soloman one day,
He answered all her questions and took her breath away!
The Queen said, "Everything I heard was true, as I sit,
Truly I had not heard the half of it!"
But foreign women gave Soloman thrills,
He worshipped their idol gods on the hills.
God said, "Your kingdom will not forever shine,
But because of David, I won't do it in your lifetime."

9-6-09

Elijah

In Israel, many worshipped and did applaud,
Baal, who was suppose to be a rain god.
Elijah told the king, "Regardless of what you heard,
There'll be no rain in years, unless I give the word."
God told Elijah, "Here's what I want you to do,
Go down by the brook and eat what the ravens bring you.
The widow was desperate, affected by the drought,
But Elijah said, "Your LAST MEAL shall not run out!"
The same widow's son later died,
Then to Elijah she cried.
Elijah prayed to God, not in strife,
And God brought the boy back to life!
After three years, there was much unrest,
Elijah said, "On Mt Carmel, it's gonna be a contest!"
Elijah asked, "How long will you straddle the fence?"
But the people remained silent, offered no defense.
So one could not tell what was their desire,
Elijah said, "The true God will bring down fire!"
Baal's prophets did all they could, but looked weak,
Elijah said, " Maybe Baal is asleep." ☺
Elijah called on God without any fanfare,
And fire from the sky filled the air.
The fire burned up everything, including the sacrifice,
As for the prophets of Baal, Elijah took their life.
Before Elijah was to be taken away,
Elisha said, "I shall not leave you this day."
When they got to the Jordan river, there was no sound,
Elijah struck the water, it parted, they crossed on dry ground!
A flaming chariot picked up Elijah, as Elisha cried,
Elijah was taken up in heaven and never died!

9-6-09

Jezebel

When the prophets of Baal were killed, Jezebel wailed,
"May the gods kill me, if I don't take your life as well."
King Ahab wanted Naboth's vineyard as an investor,
But Naboth said, "No, it's passed down from an ancestor."
The king went to bed, wouldn't eat, face to the wall,
Jezebel said, "What's the matter? What's got your gall?"
Jezebel said, "Get up, eat, don't take it so hard,
I'll get you Naboth's vineyard!
She found two scoundrels with lying breath,
They dragged out Naboth and stoned him to death.
Jezebel told Ahab, "Do you remember what I said?
You can have the vineyard now! Naboth is dead!
But they didn't know God was keeping a log,
Elijah said, "Like Naboth, your blood will be licked by dogs."
Ahab was killed by an arrow from the air,
His body taken to Samaria and buried there.
His chariot was washed by the pool, like a flood,
And the dogs came and licked the king's blood.
Jezebel painted her eye lids and fixed her hair,
Then sat at a window for all to stare.
Jehu said, "Who's on my side to be found?"
Then two or three eunuchs threw her down!
Her blood spattered the wall, payback for her deceit,
Then she was trampled under the horses feet.
Jehu said, "Someone go bury the cursed woman, a mess."
They went, but the dogs had eaten her flesh.

9-7-09

Elisha

Before Elijah approached his final hour,
Elisha asked for double his power.
Elisha saw him taken up by a chariot of fire,
And thus he did receive his desire.
Town had pretty area, but water was bad, all for naught,
Then Elisha said, "Bring me a new bowl of salt."
He poured the salt into the spring,
Then the water was good, and remained clean!
A widow owed creditors and could not toil,
All she had left was a flask of olive oil.
Elisha said, "Borrow as many pots as you can,
Then fill each one with oil, that's the plan."
With one flask, she filled them all, without running out,
God's power! That's what I'm talking about!
A Shunem woman's son had passed away,
So she went to Elisha to save the day!
Elisha went in alone, without alarm,
Stretched over the boy and his body got warm,
Elisha got up, then stretched again, and surprise!
The boy sneezed seven times and opened his eyes.
Naaman had leprosy, a body of sores,
Elisha said, "Dip seven times in the Jordan and be restored."
Naaman followed instructions, after awhile,
Then his flesh became as healthy as a young child!
In all the world, no matter where he should trod,
Naaman said, "I know now, there's no other God."

9-8-09

Hezekiah

Hezekiah did as good kings had done,
He was Zechariah's grandson.
He destroyed idols, broke the bronze serpent into bits,
Because the people had begun to worship it!
Hezekiah was twenty five when he became king,
He remained faithful to God in everything.
Assyria was crushing nations, showing no pity,
Then threatened to take Judah, Hezekiah's city.
But Isaiah said, "Proof Assyria shall meet defeat,
This year, only what grows by itself, shall you eat.
Hezekiah became sick and deathly ill,
Isaiah came to tell him God's will.
"Set your affairs in order as you lie,
You shall not recover, but surely die."
Hezekiah turned his face to the wall, praying, he wept,
"Remember oh Lord, your word I have kept."
God said, "Tell Hezekiah I've heard his prayer, seen his tears,
And to his life I will add fifteen years!"
God can not lie, always does what he says,
Hezekiah asked, "Will I be in the temple in three days?"
During this time, the sundial is how time was kept,
"Do you want it to go forward or backward ten steps?"
Hezekiah said, "It always goes forward, you see,
Make it go backwards for me.
For Hezekiah, Isaiah called on God to please,
And God made time go backward ten degrees!

9-8-09

Ezra

Ezra was a scribe, I do tell,
Who knew the law of Moses very well.
He set aside silver and gold for the Lord,
On his journey for the priest to guard.
Ezra was one of the sharpest, the people had heard,
He arrived in Jerusalem ready to spread the word!
God had protected them all their lives,
But many took pagan women as wives.
Ezra tore his clothes, pulled hair from his head and beard,
As he sat shocked and utterly in tears.
Ezra fell to his knees to pray that day,
Hoping God would forgive Israel some way.
Shecaniah confessed Israel's wrong coarse,
Said, "These pagan women, we must divorce."
"Come to Jerusalem," they were all compelled,
Or forfeit all property and be expelled.
Even leaders were guilty, and not just a few,
This all took three months to undo.

9-12-09

Nehemiah

When Nehemiah heard the wall was no longer kept,
He sat down and for days he wept.
Nehemiah prayed and on God he did lean,
"Grant success as I ask a favor from the king."
Nehemiah was a cup bearer, but did not appear glad,
So the king asked him, "Why are you so sad?"
Nehemiah's prayerful reply was not hurried,
He asked to rebuild the city where his ancestors were buried.
Nehemiah inspected the wall from gate to gate,
He knew this was a task , that could not wait.
The people came together and were on one accord,
To rebuild the wall , with the help of the Lord.
Mocked by their enemies, things looked dim,
But Nehemiah prayed and God was with him.
Indeed the wall, God would restore,
Nehemiah warned, "Stop taking from the poor!"
The people listened to what he had to say,
Because for twelve years as governor, he took no pay!
Like a team going down the field, running perfect plays,
The Israelites completed the wall in just fifty two days!
Their enemies were fearful and could only nod,
This could only have been done with the help of God.

9-13-09

Esther

Vashti's beauty shone like the sun,
Xerxes wanted to see her walk in front of everyone. ☺
The king was half drunk with wine,
He would not get his way this time.
But to prove he was right,
He banished Vashti from his sight.
To replace Vashti, was quite a contest,
The king loved Esther above all the rest.
Mordecai, her cousin, told her what to do,
"Right now, don't let them know you are a Jew."
Respect to Haman, the law did allow,
But to him, Mordecai refused to bow.
Haman was on fire, like a hot fuse,
He passed a law to kill all the Jews.
Mordecai went to Esther, seeking her help,
Said, "This is not the time to worry about self."
So Esther went to the king with her cry,
She told Mordecai, "If I die, I die."
The king couldn't sleep, ordered records to be read,
Found that if not for Mordecai, he might be dead.
Haman thought he was about to receive fanfare,
But they rode Mordecai on the king's horse, in the town square.
Haman built a gallows for Mordecai alone,
Little did he know, that it would be his own.
Esther told the king about Haman's plan,
And the king became an angry man.
The very gallows he made for Mordecai,
On it Haman, would now die.
The Jews were spared, as Mordecai assured them,
And the day is still celebrated, called Purim.

9-13-09

Mordecai

Haman was second to the king in power,
But Mordecai would become the man of the hour!
Honor and respect for Haman , was the king's plan,
However, Mordecai refused to bow to any man.
Haman learned that Mordecai was a Jew,
He decided to destroy them through and through.
Haman was as bold as he could be,
Even got the king to sign a decree.
For Mordecai, this was not good news,
It was a plot to kill all the Jews.
Mordecai asked Esther to talk to the king about the situation,
And help save the Jews from annihilation.
At first Esther refused, she didn't fully understand,
So Mordecai had to show his hand.
"If you keep quiet without a sigh,
You and all your relatives will die.
You are in a position to stop this plot,
God will save the Jews, whether you help or not."
So Esther said, "Get everyone to fast for three days,
Then I will go in and see what the king says."
Haman made a gallows on which to hang Mordecai,
He longed for the day the Jew would die.
When Esther told the king of Haman's plan,
The king became a very angry man.
The very gallows he built for Mordecai,
On it Haman himself would die.
On the kings horse Mordecai strode,
He even got to wear the king's robe.
The order to kill the Jews was struck down,
And the Jews celebrated all around!

9-23-09

34

Job

When trouble arises and you must bear a heavy load,
Take heart and remember the trials of brother Job.
The devil was searching for someone to put to the test,
God said, " Consider my servant Job, he's one of my best."
The devil said, "I really don't think he's that tough,
He should worship you, you pay him well enough!"
God spoke up for Job, told the devil he was wrong,
God said, "Go ahead , you may take all that he owns."
The Devil said , "we'll see indeed if that is the case,
When I get through with him, "he'll curse you to your face!"
When Job was told all was lost at the end of the day,
Job said, "The Lord giveth and the Lord taketh away"
But the devils head no doubt was a bit knotty,
He told God, "you didn't let me touch his body."
God said, " go ahead if that is your goal,
You can touch his body, but not his soul!"
Job became so sick, it even made his wife sigh,
She said, "Why don't you just curse God and die?"
Then with all the strength that he could summon,
Job said, "now you talking like a foolish woman."
With boils all over his body, Job didn't get out of place,
But stated, "one day I will see my Redeemer, face to face!"
However, after all the trials that Brother Job had been through,
Said, "God , when I get to heaven , I would like to talk with you.
Then God in heaven, who neither sleeps nor slumbers,
Asked Job, "Do you know each cloud by number?"
If that's not enough to impress you my friend,
God said, "where is the home of the east wind"
So you want to question God? Job thought he was ready,
But put his hand over his mouth in silence, "I said too much already."
But because of the faith that he showed,
For Brother Job, everything DOUBLE was bestowed!

Reginald Love
June 2009

Psalm 37

Don't worry about the evil doers song,
And never envy people that do wrong.
For they shall soon be cut down like grass,
Then wither like the green herb and not last.
Trust in the Lord and do as you should,
Then you shall dwell in the land and be fed good.
Delight thyself in the Lord, be set apart,
And he shall give you the desires of your heart.
Commit and trust in God in the things that you do,
Then fear not, for he shall surely help you.
He will make your innocence clear to everyone,
And the justice of your cause shine like the sun.
Be still before God and wait for him to act,
Don't worry about evil ones prospering, getting fat.
The wicked will be destroyed and not stand,
Those who trust in the Lord, will possess the land.
In a little while the wicked will disappear,
You will look for them and they won't be Here!
God's care for the innocent, he shall not sever,
And they shall receive a reward that will last forever.
They will survive when times are rough,
During a famine, they will have more than enough.
The steps of a good man are ordered by God,
And the Lord delights in his life's trod.
Though he falls, again he shall stand,
For the Lord upholds him with his hand.

10-18-09

Psalm 51

Have mercy on me, O God above,
Because of your unfailing love.
Due to your great compassion within,
I ask that you blot out the stain of my sin.
Wash me clean from my evil deed,
Purify me from my sin, I plead.
For I recognize my shameful wrong,
It haunts me all the day long.
Against thee only, I have sinned by night,
And done this evil, in thy sight.
I was born a sinner, I do believe,
And in sin, my mother did conceive.
But you desire honesty from the heart, I'm seeing,
So you can teach me to be wise in my innermost being.
Purify me from my sins and I will be clean, I know,
Wash me and I will be whiter than snow.
To have joy again, is now my choice,
You have broken me, now let me rejoice.
Create in me a clean heart, I ask of thee,
And renew the right spirit within me.
Don't banish me from where you are,
And don't take your Holy Spirit afar.
The joy of thy salvation, unto me restore,
Uphold me with thy free spirit, forever more.
Then I will teach transgressors thy ways, with glee, ☺
And sinners shall be converted unto thee.

10-18-09

Proverbs

The lips of an immoral woman will spoil,
Her mouth is sweet and smoother than oil.
Stay away from her, whatever you do,
Run from her! If you have to. ☺
She will make a man her slave,
Her steps lead straight to the grave.
To drink water from your own well is nice,
Share your love only with your wife.
The wild woman will corrupt your ways,
She'll say her husband is gone for three days.
A wise child accepts their parents rules,
While young mockers do as they choose.
The life of the Godly is full of light,
But the sinners life is black as night.
A person with good sense, bears a light load,
While a treacherous person, walks a rocky road.
A dry crust eaten in a peaceful life,
Is better that a great feast filled with strife.
Wealth makes many friends each day,
While poverty drives them away.
It is better to live alone, in the corner of an attic,
Than in a big house, with a wife who is a fanatic.
Teach your children right, from the start,
When they grow old, it will remain in their heart.

10-17-09

Isaiah

God said, "Your sins are red as scarlet, I know,
I can make them white as snow."
If a man plants a vineyard, careful, without haste,
Does he expect to get sour grapes?
But if it does, it shall cause a frown,
And then he will take the fence down.
This is the prophet Isaiah's story,
He saw the temple filled with God's glory!
Then he saw a seraphim with six wings
Place a burning coal to his lips, making him clean.
God said, "Who will bring my people in the know?"
Then Isaiah said, " Send me, I'll go!"
Tell them they shall look but not see, hear and not understand,
"They're about to experience my punishment plan."
But just as sure as a star in the east,
There's hope in the coming Prince of Peace.
He shall rule forever, just and fair,
The Messiah, king David's heir.
"One day the low and meek shall be lifted up,
And not have to drink from a bitter cup,
The crooked shall be made straight,
In the day of the Lord, I can hardly wait!
His glory shall be revealed forever,
And all flesh will see it together.
Before the world was made, God knew the score,
That one day men would study war no more.
God's word is true and shall never fade,
Every man will be under his vine and none shall be afraid.
In that day, there'll be no sun for day or moon for night,
The Lamb, the Messiah will be the glorious light!

9-24-09

Jeremiah

God said, "I knew you before you were in the womb,"
But Jeremiah thought he was too young, too soon.
God said, "Don't say that , whatever you do,
Go where I send you and do what I tell you."
The people absorbed Baal, like a noon time snack,
But God said, " I'll still take you back."
Wandering from God, was Israel's knock,
God said, " Bury the loin cloth in a rock."
It was rotted and no good , after many days,
God said, "This will be Israel, if she don't change her ways."
God said, "Go down to the potter's house and behold,
Watch him work with the clay, watch him mold.
If the clay doesn't come out like it should,
The potter can reshape it and make it good.
Jeremiah became disgusted and somewhat sore,
He said, "I won't mention God anymore."
But he found that despite the peoples wrongs,
The word was like fire, shut up in his bones!
Israel didn't heed Jeremiah or his fears,
So God said, "You'll be captive for seventy years."
Hananiah told the people only two years, he lied,
In the same year, for going against God, he died.
King Zedekiah agreed that Jeremiah was a liar,
So he was imprisoned and dropped in the mire.
This caused Ebed, an Ethiopian official, much distress,
So the king said, "Take thirty men, get him out of that mess."

9-28-09

Ezekiel

Ezekiel saw four beings hard to describe,
Each had a wheel and wings at their side.
They were very bright and not dim,
Lightening flashed back and forth between them.
With the face of a human, a lion, an eagle and an ox,
These were not beings to try to out fox!
Ezekiel had to lie for 390 days on his side,
For the sins of Israel, their greed and pride.
Then on his right side for Judah, for forty days,
A day for each year of their sins he layed.
God said, "I'm the one who gave you life,
Now you're like an unfaithful wife.
Israel time and time again, I offer you a solution,
But you choose to continue your prostitution."
God told Ezekiel, "Bring the pot to a boil,
This is Israel's fate for she hasn't been loyal."
God showed Ezekiel a valley of dry bones on the ground,
No sign of life anywhere to be found.
God said, " Can these bones live again, in fact?"
Ezekiel said, "Only you can answer that."
God said, "Speak to the bones in this way,
The Lord will bring you back to life today."
Ezekiel obeyed and spoke without fear,
A rattling across the valley, he began to hear.
This would have been a good movie score,
The bones came back together, as before!
Then Ezekiel called to the four winds,
And the bodies stood up and breathed again!
God said, "Tell Israel, they are just like these bones,
But I can bring them back again, despite their wrongs."

9-29-09

Daniel

When it comes to faith, this is what I have to say,
Brother Daniel prayed three times a day.
When captured and not wanting to be rude,
Told the King, "Thanks , but we don't want your food."
In the end when they were all put to the test,
Daniel and the Hebrew boys were better than all the rest.
The king had a dream , that he could not understand,
Little did he know, Daniel was God's right hand man!
Daniel told the king, "for seven years you will be insane,
But then God will give you back your reign.
This will be done, so that all on earth will know,
No one can rise to power, unless God says so!"
Another time , Daniel was thrown into the lions den,
Believe it or not, praying to God , was his only sin.
That night, even the king brought things to a pause,
He need not have worried, Angels gave the lions, lockjaws!
The Babylonians were partying, having a big free for all,
That is, until they saw the hand, writing on the wall.
And this was not the type of writing , one normally sees,
When the king saw it, he turned white, got weak at the knees!
The king said, " interpret it and receive riches and purple robe,"
Daniel said , I'll tell you what it says, but keep your gold.
Daniel served a God that neither sleeps nor slumbers,
Then told the king, it says, "your days in here are numbered!"
So be like Daniel, always take time out to pray,
And remember this one thing, "God don't play!"

By Reginald Love
April   2009

DANIEL PRESERVED IN THE LIONS DEN.

יהוה

When the King came to the Den, he cried with a lamentable voice unto Daniel, & said, O Daniel, servant of the living God, is thy God whom thou servest continually, able to deliver thee from the lions.

Daniel, ch. 6, v. 20.

Hosea

God told Hosea to marry a prostitute,
So he married Gomer, a woman of ill repute.
God said, "name the first child, Jezreel,
I will punish Jehu, for his wrongful kill."
God said, "name the girl Lo-ruhamah (no love),
For Israel will not be forgiven, by God above.
God said, "Name the second son Lo-ammi (not my people),
For Israel is not mine and continues her evil.
God said, "I gave Israel everything, without fail,
Yet she uses MY silver and gold to worship Baal!
God said, "Go get your wife, bring her back to you,
This I will do with Israel too."
Alcohol and prostitution had stolen Israel's brain,
They began to worship a piece of wood, that's insane!
They continue to worship idols, for goodness sake,
Israel has become no better than a half baked cake!
Israel is full of lies, deceit, and then some,
While Judah was faithful to the Holy One.
The paths of the Lord are true and right,
The righteous live by them day and night.

9-29-09

Joel

"Now listen Israel, you're going to be sad,
God's gonna send locust, you've been so bad.
The cutting locusts will have a big fest,
The swarming locusts will eat the rest.
This destruction, there will be no stopping,
Next will come the locusts hopping.
Israel will be brought to her knees,
As the locusts destroy grapevines and fig trees.
Because of Israel's evil accord,
They had nothing to offer the Lord.
The locusts appear like a mighty Army machine,
Destroying everything in front of them to be seen.
They look like tiny horses and run just as fast,
How long will their destruction last?
The earth quakes and the sun doesn't shine
God says, "Turn to me , while there is still time!"
After the locusts, there is only desolation,
Then the Lord makes a promise of restoration.
Enemy nations will have their run,
But God says, "There'll be payback, for what you've done."
The Lord's voice will be like thunder, huge,
To Israel, a fortress and welcoming refuge.

9-30-09

Amos

God said, "I see Damascus's sin, from where I sit,
Their punishment I will not forget."
The people of Gaza sin again and again, like rain,
But soon, they will feel fire and pain.
Tyre, Edom, and Ammon have sinned, not a small bit,
God said, " And I shall not forget.
Israel, from all the people on earth, I chose YOU,
I must punish the evil things you do."
"You hate honest judges , who rule,
You step on the poor, like a footstool."
God said, "I hate your show, pretense, and hypocrisy,
You religious festivals mean nothing to me."
God said, "I want to see a flood of justice, pure and clean,
And righteous living flow like a mighty stream!"
God asked Amos, "What do you see?"
He answered, " A plumbline next to thee."
God said, "I will test my people with this plumbline,
Their sins will no longer be left behind."
What did the basket of ripe fruit represent?
God said, "Israel, ripe for punishment."
When the day of judgement, fills the air,
One will be chased by a lion and met by a bear!
A trap doesn't snap shut, until it's stepped on,
Despite these warnings, Israel kept doing wrong.

9-30-09

Jonah

God told Jonah to go to Nineveh,
But Jonah didn't want to save the enemy.
Jonah took a ship going the opposite way,
But would soon find out, God don't play!
A storm arose, the ship almost went down,
Jonah was asleep, no where to be found.
The captain found Jonah down below,
Woke him and said, "Pray to the God you know."
Jonah said, "I worship God, who made the sea and land,
But right now I'm running from God's hand."
Jonah said, " Throw me into the sea,
Then it will be calm as it can be."
The men cried out to Jonah's God, Oh Lord!
Then they threw Jonah overboard.
The storm stopped at once that hour!
The sailors were amazed at God's great power.
Jonah was inside a great fish for three days,
He vowed to God to change his ways.
The great fish spit up Jonah, on the beach,
God said, "Now its time for you to preach!"
In forty days Nineveh would be destroyed,
But they changed their ways, Jonah was annoyed.
Nineveh was spared, casing Jonah to sob,
God said, "You shouldn't be angry, you did your job."

9-30-09

47

Micah

Israel kept making the wrong decisions,
So God had to send Micah some visions.
He saw God come to earth, walking on high places,
Wherever he stepped, causing melted spaces.
This was not happening because of Buddah,
But because of the sins of Israel and Judah.
On Israel, God would show no pity,
Who's to blame? Samaria, its capital city!
And Judah herself, was not very witty,
Who's to blame? Jerusalem, its capital city!
Israel lived as if there was no God,
They even took people's homes by fraud.
Because most people were concerned about self,
God gave their fields to someone else.
God tried to spare Israel the rod,
Said, "Do justly, love mercy, walk humbly with your God."
In the future the world will stop and look,
As all nations beat each spear into a pruning hook.
All wars will stop, and peace shall soar,
And men will study war no more.

10-1-09

Haggai

God was disappointed with what Israel had done,
They said, "The time to rebuild the temple hadn't come."
God said, "In your fancy homes, what are you doing?
While the Lord's house lies in ruin."
God said, "Consider how things are going for you,
Lets take a look at the things you do.
You plant much and have a fit,
Because you only harvest a little bit.
You have food to eat and drink from your cup,
But it's never enough to fill you up.
You have plenty of clothing to be worn,
But it's not enough to keep you warm.
Your money disappears, away it goes,
Like you put it in pockets filled with holes!
God said, "Consider how things are going for you,"
The Lord Almighty says, "This you should now do."
"Go up into the hills and bring down timber,
And rebuild my house, like the one I remember."

10-16-09

Zechariah

God told Zechariah to tell Israel's few,
"Return to me and I will return to you."
Zechariah in a vision during the night,
Saw riders on horses, red, brown, and white.
Israel's trouble never seem to cease,
But the riders patrolled and found the earth at peace.
Then Zechariah saw four horns one hour,
God said, "These are each a world power."
Then he saw four blacksmith in fact,
They came to give the four horns the big payback!
Then he saw a bowl of oil, on a lamp stand, of solid gold,
With two olive trees, one on each side of the bowl.
Next Zechariah saw a flying scroll,
Which banished thieves and liars, I'm told.
Israel had not been doing their best,
So God sent a woman in a basket, called wickedness.
God told Zechariah, "Judge fairly, honestly, show kindness,
And the poor, widows and orphans do not oppress.
Rejoice people of Zion! Shout in triumph, take note,
Your righteous king is coming, riding on a donkey's colt.
The world will be at peace, weapons will have no worth,
He shall reign from sea to sea , to the ends of the earth.

10-05-09

Matthew

Jesus showed that even a tax collector, he could use,
As he called Matthew to speak to the Jews.
Jesus said, "Blessed are the meek of little worth,
It is they who shall inherit the earth."
Blessed are those who thirst and hunger for God's will,
In due time they shall receive their fill.
Jesus knew adultery was in the book,
Stated, "sin can come from a lustful look."
Jesus taught it's no shame to be meek,
If you're slapped, turn the other cheek.
When you give to someone in need, don't brag,
God has already blessed you, for that be glad. ☺
Things might go better at school,
If students were taught the golden rule.
Like a robber caught on tape, with the loot,
You can identify a tree, by its fruit.
The Roman officer said, "I'm not worthy, just say the word."
Jesus said, "In Israel faith such as this, I have not heard."
Some don't understand God or fear,
Jesus said, "He who hath ears, let him hear."
Who am I? Jesus asked, some disciples gave a nod,
But Peter said, "You're the Messiah, son of the living God."

10-6-09

My Redeemer

I like the Lakers, the Sooners, and the Cowboys!
But it's about my Redeemer, that I wanna make some noise!
With John the Baptist, into the water , Jesus eased,
God said, "this is my beloved son, in whom I'm well pleased"
A young man from birth, was as blind as he could be,
Good or bad? All I know, is I was blind and now I see!
Martha was disappointed, mournful, and out of sorts,
Until she heard my Redeemer say, " Lazarus come forth!"
When the storm was raging, it broke the disciples will,
Until my Redeemer came forth and said, "peace be still."
So if you want a saviour, Father, Mother, Son or Daughter,
I give you my Redeemer, "who walked on water!"
So even if your team never wins the Super Bowl,
I give you my Redeemer, "who can save your soul!"
When they hung Jesus on the cross, some thought all was lost,
Little did they know, for mankind , he was paying the cost.
In the 9th hour it got dark and the earth shook, where he had trod,
The centurion said, "Surely! This must have been the Son of God!"
They placed him in tomb, but they knew what the scriptures said,
That in three days, the Messiah would be raised from the dead.
On Sunday morning, the angel revealed the master plan,
My Redeemer had risen! With all power in his hands!

January 2009

Peter

Peter walked on water, not to please us,
But started sinking, when he took his eyes off Jesus.
Jesus was arrested, according to the scripture plan,
When questioned, Peter said, "I don't know the man!"
On the day of Pentecost many could not perceive,
But Peter preached and three thousand came to believe!
At the beautiful gate, Peter heard a crippled beggar talk,
Peter said, "In the name of Jesus, get up and walk!"
Peter and the apostles were put in jail,
But an angel opened the gates without fail.
Peter had a vision of a four cornered large sheet,
Filled with animals, he thought not good to eat.
Then he saw the vision three times, before it was done,
It became clear to Peter, God's love was for everyone.
Trials are only to test your faith and soul,
They purify like fire purifies gold.
Our lives, God is able to cleanse,
His love covers a multitude of sins.
The day of judgment, some will not cherish,
For many ungodly people will perish.
Peter was a bold apostle as could be found,
He even asked to be crucified upside down.

10-7-09

Elizabeth

Elizabeth was Zechariah's wife,
They both tried to live a Godly life,
There were no children between them, we're told,
And by now , they were both very old.
An angel told her husband, she would have a son,
But Zechariah did not believe it could be done.
However the angel was Gabriel, not one to scorn,
Told Zechariah, "You will not speak, until the child is born."
"How kind the Lord is," Elizabeth exclaimed,
"He has taken away my disgrace and shame."
Mary came to visit Elizabeth soon,
And Elizabeth's child, leaped in her womb!
When the baby was born, it was a boy,
Neighbors and relatives showed their joy. ☺
Of his fathers name , they were fond,
But Elizabeth said , "No , his name is John."
So they asked the father his name plan,
He wrote John, and could speak again!

10-8-09

Mary

In an appearance that was somewhat scary,
The angel, Gabriel, appeared to mary.
There's no need to be afraid of me,
You're highly favored, God is going to bless thee.
"You're going to have a baby," the angel didn't lie,
He will be great and called the son of the most high.
Mary then asked Gabriel about his plan,
"How can this be? I haven't been with a man."
Gabriel said, "The Holy Spirit will overshadow you solely,
Therefore the baby born to you will be holy."
Mary said, "I'm the Lord's servant, I accept what I've heard,
May everything happen, according to your word."
When her fiancé found out, he knew not what to say,
But decided to get rid of her in a private way.
An angel appeared to Joseph in a dream,
To explain what all this did mean.
"Don't be afraid to marry Mary, it's not like you believe,
It was by the Holy Spirit that she did conceive.
And just as the angel did warn,
Mary remained a virgin, till Jesus was born.

10-10-09

John The Baptist

Over four hundred years, no prophet for the day,
Then John the Baptist, came to pave the way.
His look probably made some people stare,
His clothes were made from camel hair.
He wasn't a person with a lot of money,
For food, he ate locusts and wild honey.
People from Jerusalem, Judea and Jordan, he did reach,
For they came out to the wilderness to hear him preach.
He baptized with water and did not tire,
But said, "One is coming who will baptize with fire."
This John made sure not to confuse,
And said, "I'm not even worthy to carry his shoes."
The baptism of Jesus, John did not want to do,
And told Jesus, "I should be baptized by you."
With John the Baptist, into the water, Jesus eased,
God said, "This is my beloved son, in whom I'm well pleased."
John sent two disciples to Jesus, booking!
To ask, "Are you the Messiah? Or do we keep looking?"
Jesus said, "Tell John the lame walk, the deaf hear, blind see,
God bless those who are not offended by me."
John caused Herod very much strife,
Told him it was wrong to marry his brother's wife.
John's words to Herod would disturb,
Even so, Herod like to hear John's word.
Herodias's dance made Herod offer a referendum,
"Ask for anything you want, even half my kingdom!"
Her mother didn't like what John had said,
She told her to ask for John the Baptist's head.
Jesus said of John the Baptist later,
"Of men born, there are none greater."

10-10-09

58

Blessed
are those who
have not seen and yet
have believed. *John 20:29*

Stephen

Christians should be shining beacons,
Like Stephen, one of the first deacons.
This was during the Church's early days,
Stephen did miracles that did amaze!
Some Jews must have thought Stephen a joke,
But none could stand the wisdom by which he spoke.
So they lied on Stephen because of spite,
Stephen's face, like an angels, became very bright!
Stephen in reply, began to quote scripture,
From Moses to Jesus, trying to paint a picture.
This was Stephen's final stand,
He saw Jesus standing at God's right hand.
Stephen tried to tell them about this sight,
But they covered their ears in fright.
So they drug him out to stone him after all,
And some laid their coats at the feet of Saul.
Stephen said, "God don't charge them with this sin."
Stephen was stoned to death then.

10-13-09

Paul

Saul traveled to Damascus, on the plains,
His task was to bring Christians back in chains.
But on his way, he saw a light, as bright as it could be,
Then heard a voice, "Why are you persecuting me?"
Saul asked, "Who are you sir? Without refuting,
The voice said, "I'm Jesus, the one you're persecuting!"
Aninias did not want to see Saul during this while,
But God said, "He will spread my word to the Gentiles."
Elymas the sorcerer thought he was one of a kind,
But Paul looked him in the eye and made Elymas blind.
Paul preached where the spirit led,
But the Jews stoned him and left him for dead.
As believers stood around showing pity,
Paul got up and went back into the city!
In Athens Paul said, "You have an alter to the unknown god,
To tell you who he is, that's my job!
After being arrested, Paul presented his defense plea,
Even King Agrippa said, "Paul thou almost persuadest me."
In Rome, Paul was put to the test,
He got private lodging, but house arrest.
People who say there is no God, have lied,
From the beginning, God put it innately on their inside.
Nothing can separate us from God's love cord,
Which can be found in Christ Jesus our Lord.

10-14-09

Cornelius

In caesara there was a Roman Officer, I must tell,
Who was a devout man and feared the God of Israel.
He gave generously to charity, very fair,
And regularly, he was a man of prayer.
He saw a vision of an angel approaching,
The angel said, "Your prayers and gifts, God's been noticing."
"Send for the apostle Peter to come your way,
Then listen to what he has to say."
Then Peter's vision he had, to him was now clear,
God loves all races, that hold him dear.
Peter preached to them the Good news,
Glad that he was someone God could use.
In them there was found to be no guile,
As the Holy Spirit was poured out on the Gentiles.
The truth, they now realized,
So Peter gave orders for them to be baptized.
Many Jews didn't like what Peter had done,
So he had to explain to them, his VISION.

10-15-09

Nathaniel

Called by Jesus, Philip was ready to shout,
Told Nathaniel, "We've found who the prophets wrote about."
"He is Jesus, from the Nazareth city,
Nathaniel asked, "Can any good come from a place of pity?"
Philip was excited and filled with glee, ☺
So he told Nathaniel, "You just come and see."
Philip and Nathaniel approached Jesus after awhile,
Jesus said, "An Israelite indeed, in whom is no guile."
Nathaniel asked, "How do you know this about me?"
Jesus said, "I knew you before Philip saw you at the fig tree."
Nathaniel then acknowledged with a nod,
"Rabbi, you are truly the son of God."
Jesus said, "Because of this, you believe me?
Greater things that this, shall you see."
"You will see heaven open up and understand,
Angels ascending and descending on the son of man."

10-16-09

Nicodemus

A religious leader, Nicodemus was a Pharisee,
But it was Jesus he came to see.
Whether it was out of fear or fright,
We know he came to Jesus by night.
He said, "Teacher, by the miracles that you do,
We all know that God is with you."
Jesus gave him a new referendum,
"You must be born again, to see the kingdom."
This saying , Nicodemus did not understand,
He asked, "Can a man enter the womb again?"
This was his confusion, Jesus tried to clear it,
"You must be born of the flesh and the spirit."
"Humans can only reproduce humans, that's right,
But the Holy Spirit gives life, that's out of sight!" ☺
"You can't tell where it comes from, but you hear the wind,
So don't be surprised, you MUST be born again."
Nicodemus was a respected Jewish teacher, an educated man,
Yet, this teaching, he did not understand.
Jesus said, "As the bronze serpent was lifted on a pole,
I must be lifted up, to make men whole."

10-16-09

Dorcas

Dorcas was a believer, in God she did fear,
She was a doer of the word, not just a hearer.
She was always giving and doing more,
Kind things for others and helping the poor.
She became ill, died and there was much gloom,
Her friends prepared her body and put her in an upper room.
They heard that Peter was nearby, not far away,
So they sent for him, "Please come without delay."
They took Peter to the room, where Dorcas layed,
The women wept and showed coats she had made.
Peter asked them all to leave the room,
They would see the power of prayer, real soon!
This was not a twist of fate or good luck,
Peter knelt and PRAYED, then said, "Dorcas get up!"
To the believer, this is not a surprise,
Dorcas sat up and opened her eyes!
Peter called in the widows, showed what was achieved,
The news spread and then, in GOD, many believed.

10-16-09

James

Just as the sun rises and burns up the grass,
Wealthy people will fade away and not last.
For those who endure testing and strife,
God has promised them a crown of life.
No one can say, God tempted them to do sin,
This comes from their OWN evil desires within.
True religion is not worthless, like a bubble,
Real Christians help orphans and widows in trouble.
In fancy clothes, rich people may be clad,
But it's no reason to treat your poor guest bad.
And if you forget all that James has said,
Remember, "Faith without works is dead."
Control your tongue and watch what you say,
Then you will control yourself in every other way.
This is a rule James tried to exert,
Because the small tongue, can cause a lot of hurt.
To humble one's self, is the thing to do,
Resist the devil and he will flee from you.
Remember you are of the chosen few,
Draw close to God and God will draw close to you.
The fervent prayer of a righteous man availeth much,
It's God's way of saying, "Keep in touch." ☺

10-16-09

Satan

The devil was an archangel and looked good,
But he stopped acting like an angel should.
He was created perfect, so it is somewhat strange,
That he himself, created this evil change.
The devil had pride, wanted to be equal with God,
A fatal path that he chose to trod.
In heaven there was a great war,
Like none that we have seen thus far.
Michael and his angels defeated the devil, kicked him out,
Then in all of heaven, there was a great shout!
The devil was thrown down to earth,
And for years, he did terror and curse.
In the Garden of Eden, Satan did deceive,
And has caused many others not to believe.
When Christ returns, he will end all fears,
Satan will be locked up, for a thousand years.
The devil will be loosed for a season,
And will fool many, who lack reason.
They surrounded God's people and the beloved city,
But fire from heaven, came down, showing them no pity.
The devil was proven to be a liar,
And he was thrown into the lake of fire.
This would be the final sever,
There he will be tormented, day and night, forever!

10-18-09

The New Heaven

John saw a new heaven and a new earth,
For the old was gone, of no more worth.
He saw the holy city, coming down like a pretty bride,
Then from the throne a shout of pride.
Look! The home of God is with his people!
No more sorrows and no more evil.
The Lamb said, "I'm Alpha and Omega, the beginning and the end,
Those who are thirsty, I will bless to no end.
An angel told John, "Let me show you the bride,
The wife that will be the Lamb's pride.
It was filled with the glory of God so near,
And looked like a gem of jasper, crystal clear.
It had twelve gates, that you could tell,
On each, was written one of the tribes of Israel.
There were twelve gates on each side, east, west, north and south,
A sight no doubt, that would close one's mouth.
An angel with a gold measuring stick, measured it right there,
Imagine this, he found it to be a perfect square!
What will it be like to see the New Heaven at last?
With walls of Jasper, streets of gold, clear as glass.
The twelve gates were each a single pearl,
It must have looked like nothing of this world!
Then John, who was still on his feet,
Saw a crystal river flowing down main street!
There will be no more sorrow, no more strife,
On each side of the river, a tree of life.
The city won't need the sun for day or the moon for night,
The glory of God and the Lamb, will be its light!
Jesus said, "My angel brought this message from afar,
I am the source of David, the Bright Morning Star.

10-18-09

I Cried

I knew it was coming, seeing results come in, I sit and sighed,
But when they announced Obama then winner, I Cried.
Daddy, Big Mamma and others did not live to see,
Nov 4, 2008, a major day in American history!
Not knowing what to say or do,
With tears in my eyes, said "Obama I'm proud of you!"
I thought about how when this nation was formed,
Blacks were slaves, ridiculed, murdered and scorned.
The road to freedom was not easy, but many tried,
When I thought of their hardships, I Cried.
I looked as many laughed, yelled and jumped to their feet,
But I thought about all the years, we had to take the back seat.
I thought about Jane Pittman's son taken from her side,
He was killed for no reason, and I Cried.
I thought about, "Death in a Promised Land" Tulsa, 1921,
When thousands of Blacks were killed, one by one.
I thought about Martin, Bobby, and JFK,
If only they could have lived to see this day.
I thought about Alabama, Selma to Montgomery,
And the marchers who survived "Bloody Sunday.
I was overjoyed with tears, but crying still,
As I thought about the death of Emmett Till.
I'm proud of Obama, but when I thought of all who died,
I sit there alone in my front room, and I Cried.
We now can play any sport, attend any school, but don't be content!
Because at long last, a Black man is now President.

July 2009
Reginald Love

About the Author

Reginald Love was born in Tulsa, Oklahoma, March 17, 1957. When he was five years old, his father, a construction worker, was involved in an accident, that left him disabled. The family then moved to a remote rural area in the southeastern part of the state, known as Bluff, Oklahoma. After attending Lincoln Elementary in the first and second grade, a segregated school, he then attended school in Soper from the third grade till graduating from high school. He was the Salutatorian of his Junior High Class. In high school, he played baseball and basketball, graduated third in the class and was nominated by then, Speaker of The House, Carl Albert to attend West Point. In 1976 he was listed in Who's Who Among Junior College students, as he was on the dean's honor roll, varsity basketball team, and president of the African American Club. He received an ROTC scholarship and graduated from Oklahoma State University, with a B.S. in Health and Physical Education, and also as a Second Lieutenant in the U.S. Army. He received Army Commendation Medals as a Mortar Platoon Leader and Tank Platoon Leader. He became clean and sober in 1988. He is a physical education teacher and enjoys bowling, fishing, working out and playing, as well as coaching baseball and basketball.

CPSIA information can be obtained
at www.ICGtesting.com
Printed in the USA
FSOW02n1658010317
31409FS

9 781449 055738